Why Men Have Hairy Bums

And Othe

By

Viv Wade

Edited by Joely Wade.

Images courtesy of Pixabay.com

ISBN- 13: 978-1544225159

ISBN- 10: 1544225156

Contents

If you've ever wondered why men's bums are hairy, here's one theory...

WHY MEN HAVE HAIRY BUMS

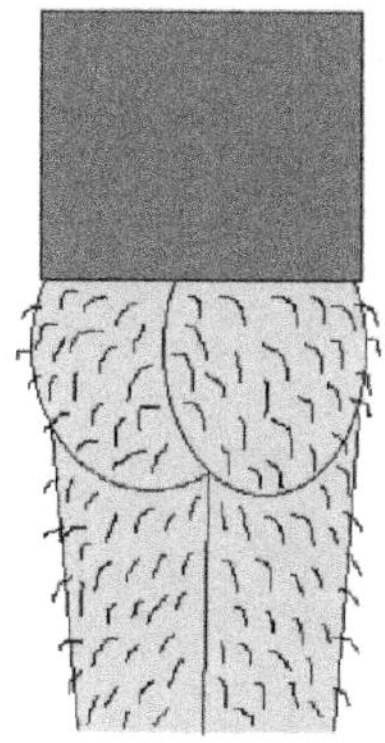

The Bible says, so I believe,
That God wanted to punish Eve,
Because in Eden one fine day,
She led her man Adam astray.

So after God created man,
He added something to his plan.
He said, "And it shall come to pass,
That man shall have a hairy ass.
Then in cold weather, or a storm,
A furry coat will keep it warm.
I also think it will look neat
To give them all a hirsute seat."

But what had God also foreseen?
A hairy bum is hard to clean!
It's plain to see, if you should glance
At your bloke's unwashed underpants.

No matter how much he may wipe,
He always leaves a dirty stripe.

So women suffer to this day,
Because Eve led Adam astray,
For in most households, I suppose,
The *woman* has to wash the clothes.
She sorts the laundry in despair
At all his filthy underwear.

Undies with skid marks are no joke,
She has to give them a good soak.
It's hard to get those soiled pants clean.
Thank God for the washing machine!

I seem to keep acquiring stray cats - I've got three at the moment, plus another couple that visit from time to time. Someone my husband works with has 18 of them! So it inspired me to write this poem...

A MULTITUDE OF MOGGIES

A cat came to my house one day,
He looked too thin, he was a stray.
He seemed so sad out in the street.
I gave him some tuna to eat,
Then when he'd eaten a whole tin,
He seemed to think he should come in.

He darted through my open door,
Left mucky paw prints on the floor.
He looked round with a lordly stare,
Then settled in my comfy chair.
He looked at me as if to say,
"I live here now, I'm here to stay!"

Soon after that, another stray
Arrived at my front door one day.

His fur was sparse, his ears were torn,
He looked neglected and forlorn.
I felt I had to give him food;
To not feed him would have been rude.
I opened up a tin of fish,
And fed it to him, on a dish.
He fixed me with his catty grin,
Before I knew it, he'd moved in.
He gave a small, contented shrug,
And settled down upon the rug.

I think those two cats sent word round
About the soft touch they had found.
Loads of cats began to arrive,
They formed a queue along the drive,
And with a caterwauling din
Demanded that I let them in!

Now I must buy food in large vats
To feed all of those pampered cats.
They cost a small fortune to keep,
They won't eat anything that's cheap!
Those spoilt cats aren't even grateful
For each tasty bowl and plateful.

They don't respect me, it's quite plain,
They treat me with haughty disdain.
They bring in half-dead birds and mice,
Which really is not very nice!
They sleep in cupboards, and in drawers,
My rugs are shredded by their claws.

The house is covered in cat hair,
Six cats sit upon every chair.
It seems there is no room for me,
My house is now a cattery.
They've even commandeered my bed -
I've had to move into the shed!

The perfect way to relax...

ODE TO A BATH

To ease your bones, and soothe your wrath,
Relax into a nice hot bath.
When life fills you with cares and woes,
Turn on the taps, take off your clothes.
Some bubble bath, a glass of wine,
I guarantee you'll soon feel fine.
Until some pest comes to spoil it,
"Mom! I need to use the toilet!"

I saw a TV documentary a while back, about men who had blow-up dolls as companions. They treated them like real women, they dressed them up, and even took them out on dates. I don't know if it was because they couldn't find a real woman, or they just thought a plastic one would be easier to live with! It inspired me to write this poem...

INFLATABLE IRENE

I'm Inflatable Irene, your blow-up girlfriend.
I am here when you need me, weekday or weekend.
I don't need gifts, or flowers, or candlelit meals,
And I'll never be taller than you in high heels.

I'm Inflatable Irene, your rubber romance.
I can make you so happy, just give me a chance.
I will never get fat round the thighs, or the rump,
Unless you go too far with the bicycle pump.

I'm Inflatable Irene, your PVC peach.
I'm not out of your league, I am within your reach.
I will never grow old, I won't let myself go.
If you'd like my boobs bigger, just give them a blow.

I'm Inflatable Irene, your plastic princess.
I will wear what you like, lingerie or a dress.
I will never be moody, I won't slap your face.
When you go on vacation, I'll fit in your case.

I'm Inflatable Irene, your babe-shaped balloon.
I won't mind if you don't want to cuddle, or spoon.
I will never stop loving you, I'll always care.
I won't tell you you're too fat, or laugh at your hair.

I'm Inflatable Irene, your air-filled air-head.
If you are feeling frisky, just take me to bed.
I won't be disappointed, no matter how quick.
You don't need to be gentle, my rubber's quite thick.

I'm Inflatable Irene, your polythene pal.
Whatever you're into, I am your kinda gal.
When you're bored of me, kill me - a knife through my heart.
I won't cry out for help, I'll just give one long *fart...*

This is a poem about one of my favourite foods...

ODE TO A BACON SANDWICH

One food I'd eat for every course
Is bacon sarnies with brown sauce.
There is no scent quite as thrilling
As smoked bacon rashers grilling!

Some people say that it's cruel
To eat animals for fuel.
And eating flesh does seem vicious,
But crisp bacon's *so* delicious!

Yet I would like to make amends
To our remaining porcine friends.
So when I die, and cease to be,
Just let the porky pigs eat *me!*

The trouble with buying a new piece of furniture is it makes all your old stuff look shabby...

THE NEW SOFA

Our sofa had grown shabby, it was looking past its prime.
And so, we both decided it was sofa-shopping time.
We went in lots of shops, as we searched for the sort of couch
That looked like one on which we could both comfortably slouch.
Until at last, we found a stylish leather one, in brown,
Located in a warehouse on the other side of town.
Although it was expensive, we felt it was worth the price.
Besides, it was the only one we *both* agreed was nice!
And so, we paid the money, and were pleased to hear them say
We would not have to wait long, they would bring it the next day.

So early the next morning, we saw a big van arrive,
And watched as two strong men carried the sofa up the drive.
They brought it in, and placed it in the middle of the room.
But as we both admired it, well, my face was filled with gloom.
For though our brand-new sofa was as stylish as we'd thought,
It made our other furniture look old. Shabby, in short.

I said, "That nice new sofa makes the carpet look threadbare,
It's looking rather dingy, it's had too much wear and tear.
It was nice when we bought it, but it is not anymore.
I think we need to buy another carpet, for this floor."
So, we bought a new carpet, an expensive one, in beige.
The one the salesman said was now in vogue, and all the rage.
But when it had been fitted, I said, "Oh dear, there's a catch,
We'll need to buy new curtains, for those old ones just don't match!"

So, we bought a pair of curtains, and hung them on the rail,
But as I looked around the room, my face began to pale.
I said, "Oh, that old sideboard does not look right now, you know,
It does not match our new stuff. I'm afraid it has to go!"
So, we bought a new sideboard, and replaced our old TV.
We bought a new light fitting, and an ornament, or three.
But as we hung a brand-new gilt-framed mirror on the wall,
I looked at the wallpaper, and said, "This won't do at all!
This paper is *so* dated, it will *have* to be replaced!
We need to buy some new wallpaper, and a load of paste."

So, we re-papered the walls, painted the doors and ceiling,
But after we had finished, I said, "I have a feeling
The wallpaper we've chosen does not go with the settee..."
And that was when my husband told me he was leaving me!

I saw a report a while back, which said that people tended to be happier if they quit Facebook, as using the site causes them to constantly compare their own life with the seemingly perfect lives of their Facebook friends, which leads to feelings of dissatisfaction. It inspired me to write this poem...

I WISH LIFE WAS LIKE FACEBOOK

I wish life was like Facebook, where everyone is happy,
And every day is such fun, and not boring, or crappy.
Just look at all the photos, with all those smiling faces.
Never-ending holidays in interesting places.

It's easy to make Facebook friends with everyone you meet.
In real life, people ignore you when walking down the street.
But you'll find lots of online pals, who'll want to 'add' you, too.
Then they can feel so smug if they have loads more friends than you.

On Facebook, people look so great in every pic and snap,
You never see a photo where they really look like crap.
You see them knocking back booze with mates, all fun and laughter.
But you will never see how they look the morning after.

You see them at social events, and far-flung, sandy shores.
They never seem to go to work, or do the household chores.
They're always dressed to look their best, poised, in flattering pose.
You never see them look a mess, or sat picking their nose.

Are they really all as happy as their profiles reveal?
If people want to share their lives, I wish they'd keep it real!
Let's start an 'honest' Facebook trend, and here's where it begins.
Check my new profile picture. There's me - putting out the bins!

I sometimes get annoyed with the pigeons in my garden, because they take all the food I put out on the bird feeder, and the smaller birds don't get any. My neighbours must think I'm mad, because I often run outside clapping my hands to try to scare the pigeons away! I've even tried squirting them with water, but as soon as I go inside, they're back on the bird feeder. So it inspired me to write this poem...

THE GREEDY PIGEON

There's a feeder in my garden,
And when the ground starts to harden
I put out lots of tasty seed,
So the small birds can have a feed.
I also put out scraps and crumbs,
But then the Greedy Pigeon comes.
To scare the sparrow and the tit,
He flaps his wings - aggressive git!

I've never seen a bird so fat,
That pigeon's bigger than a cat!
It is a wonder he can fly.
A selfish look is in his eye,

He opens his enormous beak,
And eats enough food for a week.
He gobbles, fast as he's able,
Till no food's left on the table.
Then with a satisfying burp,
He leaves a tip, the filthy twerp.
He treats the table like a loo,
And leaves a pile of pigeon poo!

He cares not if he gives offence,
As he flies off over the fence.
His appetite is quite obscene,
It angers me that he's so mean.
I would not begrudge him a share,
But he takes all, and that's not fair.
He does not leave the smallest bit,
To feed the sparrow, or the tit.

That pigeon thinks he's so clever.
He won't have his way for ever -
I'll punish him for all his greed,
Next time he comes to have a feed.
To put a stop to all his fun,
I'll blast him with my water gun,
Then when he is too wet to fly,
I'll put him in a pigeon pie!

The small birds will be glad, I trust,
When he's beneath a pastry crust.
I'll put out the leftover crumbs
For any little bird that comes.
A fitting end to the drama,
What you might call 'pigeon karma'!

These days we are always being told what we should and shouldn't eat, and sometimes it gets a bit confusing, as the advice is often contradictory. I also get a bit annoyed when a medical professional tries to lecture me about diet and exercise, and they're more unfit than I am! So it inspired me to write this poem...

FIVE-A-DAY

These days, the doctors like to say
That we should eat our five-a-day.
Cut down on sugar, salt and fat,
No cakes or biscuits - none of that.
Stop smoking, and ease off the drink,
If you wish to stay in the pink.
Walk everywhere, don't take the car,
And jog to work, it's not that far.

But if we take all their advice,
Then life no longer seems so nice.
Eating veg is not that easy,
Brussels sprouts make me feel queasy.
Though salad may reduce my hips,
My body's craving fish and chips.

And nothing can lift up my mood
Like snacking on unhealthy food.

It's so easy to get confused
Which foods should and should not be used.
I think those doctors are all fools,
They're constantly changing the rules.
Years ago, it was understood
That dairy foods would do you good,
But now they say they won't digest,
And drinking soya milk is best.

"Eat fruit!" they said, smug and placid,
Now fruit rots your teeth with acid.
Then eggs were fine, then they were not,
I think they may have lost the plot!
It's quite hard to make up my mind
Which foods are bad, and which are kind,
And why should I heed what they say,
When it changes from day to day?

My Doctor told me to get fit,
But he is such a hypocrite.
He just drove past me in his Jag,
Whilst puffing on a high-tar fag.
And he should really lose some weight,
His BMI is 58!
I think he should leave me alone
Until he's lost at least 6 stone.

Will healthy food make us stronger,
Or will life just *seem* much longer?

Good diet is no guarantee
That you'll achieve longevity.
For you could go through all that fuss,
Then get run over by a bus.
It's down to luck, no one can say
The age at which you'll pass away.

A girl I knew went for a jog,
And drowned when she fell in a bog.
Whilst 90-year-old Mr Hinks,
Eats what he likes, and smokes, and drinks.
Why make your life a misery
To try to live to 93?
Those doctors can all take a hike,
I'm going to eat what I like!

Like most people, I hate putting together flat-pack furniture. There always seems to be at least one piece missing, or bits of it are damaged. I particularly hate flat-pack furniture from Ikea, as I have found their customer service department to be really awful! So this poem is based on an experience I had a while back...

THE FLAT-PACK FURNITURE FIASCO

I thought I'd turn the spare room into somewhere I can write.
I cleared my husband's rubbish out, and painted the walls white,
I laid a rug upon the floor, put up a roller blind
In neutral tones that won't distract my literary mind.

The next items I needed were a sturdy desk and chair,
And a bookcase for displaying all my bestsellers there.
So there was no avoiding it, the solution was clear,
I would need a shopping trip – a visit to Ikea.

It's not somewhere I like to shop, it covers too much ground,
You can't go straight to what you want, you have to walk all round.
I made the two-mile journey – *twelve hours later* I got back.
I'd bought some office furniture, all flattened in a pack.

I ripped the cardboard open, and I laid out all the parts,
The flimsy Allen keys, and ninety-page instruction charts.
The directions were in languages that I cannot speak;
None of it was in English, only Sanskrit, Welsh and Greek.

I looked at all the diagrams, but none of them made sense.
I know I'm not an idiot, but they made me feel dense!
I tried to make the parts fit every which way that I could,
The screw holes did not line up, and the fixings were no good.

The Allen keys kept bending, and the grommets weren't all there,
The screws were the wrong size, and bits were broken off the chair.
Well, after I had sweated, and worked hard for many hours,
I gave up. That crap furniture was beyond my powers!

I gathered all the pieces, and returned them to the store,
And said, "This stuff is rubbish - I don't want it anymore!
Your furniture is shoddy, not the standard I'd expect.
Ikea, you can ***'go away*** " (or words to that effect).

I went home, and I walked into the spare room, now so bare,
And sat down on the rug, because I did not have a chair.
I had a little cry, and then I went down to the shed,
And found a camping table, and an old deckchair in red.

I put them in the spare room, found a crate to store my books,
So now I've everything I need - I don't care how it looks!
My laptop's on the table, and I'm seated in the chair,
No bestsellers in the crate... maybe one day, they'll be there!

Who needs flat-pack furniture to have a good idea?
A deckchair's fine for writing - so kiss my butt, Ikea!

This is a poem about someone who found himself in the wrong place, at the wrong time...

THE BURGLAR

I am a burglar by trade,
Quite a fortune I have made,
Stealing people's bits and bobs,
While they're out, doing their jobs.
Well, it beats going to work,
Like an ordinary jerk.
The tax man can't bother me,
And I pay no VAT.

Well, one day, I saw a house
Near the pub, The Dog & Grouse.
It was big, and rather posh,
Obviously full of dosh.
So I hatched a little plan,
Whereby I would be the man
To relieve them of their cash,
In and out, quick as a flash.

I would come when it was dark,
Hang around outside the park,
And I'd have a little scout
To make sure they had gone out.
Then I'd sneak round to the back,
Shove my jemmy in a crack,
Then I would let myself in,
So I could do some burglin'.

I went back later that night,
When the moon was shining bright.
I surveyed that big, posh house,
All was quiet as a mouse.
There were no lights on at all,
In the front room, or the hall.
I was left without a doubt
That the owners had gone out.

So I nipped round to the back,
Took the jemmy from my sack,
And I prised open the door,
Like a hundred times before.
In the dark, I found the hall,
Slid my hand along the wall,
Till the handle of a door
Brushed against my thieving paw.

So I crept across the floor,
And I pushed open the door.
I tiptoed into the room,
No presentiment of doom.
As my hand reached for the light,
Well, I nearly died of fright!

Sudden brightness met my eyes,
Then a loud cry of "SURPRISE!"

As I looked around the room,
Well, my heart was filled with gloom,
For surrounding me I saw
Some officers of the law -
Round about fifty, or so!
How could I possibly know
That the house I'd tried to fleece
Would be full of the police?

'Twas a party for their boss,
Chief Superintendent Moss,
Who'd decided to retire
From his career with the Shire.
I had not known that the house
Belonged to Moss and his spouse.
As I perceived my mistake,
Both my knees began to shake.

So I turned around to leave,
But a copper grabbed my sleeve,
And he said, "The house you've picked,
Was a big mistake - you're nicked!"
And just then, in came the Chief,
His eyes wide with disbelief.
He said, "What a nice surprise,
A retirement bash - thanks, guys!"

Then he said, "Hello, hello!
Here's a face that I don't know!"

When the cops told him the fact
They had caught me in the act
Of trying to nick his stuff,
He said, "Oh dear, that *is* rough!
Any other house you'd picked,
And you might not have been nicked.
But you've made an epic fail,
So for you, my lad, it's jail!
But first, you will have to wait,
For I want to celebrate!"

Then they tied me to a chair,
And they forced me to sit there
While they drank, and ate nice food,
And enjoyed the party mood.
They did not give me one bite,
Nor a beverage, all night.
And then early the next morn,
A police car came at dawn.

They took me down to a cell,
With a very nasty smell.
As I heard them turn the key,
How I wanted to be free!
But I knew that I was trapped,
All my energy was sapped.
I know it's true what they say,
A life of crime does not pay.
Now I sit here, in the clink,
With nothing to do, but think
What an idiot I've been
To end up in Winson Green*!

**Winson Green is a prison, in Birmingham.*

This short poem is about my favourite remedy for depression...

ODE TO CHOCOLATE

When I feel sad, one thing helps me -
Chocolate made by Cadbury.
When all my plans start to unfurl,
I tuck into a lovely Twirl.
If life feels like one big mistake,
I chow down on a crumbly Flake.
I don't need diamonds, or silk,
As long as I've got Dairy Milk.
That soothing taste cures all distress,
Though soon I'll need a larger dress...

In my earlier book, 'Things Can Only Get Verse', I wrote a poem called 'Flatulent Freddy's Flying Machine', about a man who built a fart-powered plane. This is a sequel to that poem...

FLATULENT FREDDY FLIES AGAIN

After Fred built his aeroplane,
He thought he'd like to try again,
To find another way to fly,
Fart-powered, high into the sky.
Some people thought he was insane
To build a plane run on methane,
But Freddy did not care one jot -
Why not use power from his bot?
And so, one sunny afternoon,
He built his own hot air balloon!

Fred went out shopping for some fags,
And a large roll of strong bin bags.
When fixed together with duct tape,
The bin bags started to take shape.
Fred worked hard all that afternoon,
Until he'd made a large balloon.

"What's next?" asked Fred, sucking his teeth,
"A basket to go underneath!"
Fred went to his brother's camper,
And borrowed a picnic hamper.
He attached it with some clothes line,
And thought his balloon looked just fine!
"So now," said Fred, "It has to be,
Some Three Bean Curry, for my tea!"

So, Fred went to his mother's house,
Because he did not have a spouse,
And Mummy cooked a great big pan
Of curry for her little man.
She served it to him on a plate,
Then Freddy sat and ate, and ate.
And after only half an hour,
His bum was full of wind-power!

Fred bid his mum a fond farewell,
He went outside, and ran like hell.
When he reached his hot air balloon,
He climbed aboard, and very soon,
With power spurting from his ass,
The balloon filled with bottom-gas.
Fred farted like a jet engine!
And so the balloon did begin
To rise up, high above the trees,
Powered by Freddy's botty-breeze.

Fred floated on for quite some time
Over the town. It was sublime!
He felt like such a clever boy,
And so, to celebrate his joy,

Fred reached into his duffel bag,
To get some matches, and a fag...

Fred never got to light his fag,
And take a satisfying drag.
As soon as he had struck the light,
His bum-gas started to ignite!
A ***FLASH!*** A ***BANG!*** A ***WHIZZ!*** And soon,
Poor Fred was heading for the moon!

Since that day, no one has seen Fred.
He is still missing, presumed dead.
But yet, there is a ray of hope.
If you peer through a telescope
Towards the surface of the moon,
You'll see a small hot air balloon!

I think our Freddy's still alive,
He's clever enough to survive.
And I'm sure he will find a way
To come back down to Earth one day.
Maybe Fred will build a rocket,
Run on gas from his back pocket.
Though, his poor mother must worry,
How she'll deliver his curry!

What's the best remedy for a broken heart...?

LOST LOVE

When I was young, I fell in love,
He seemed sent from heaven above.
His eyes were blue, his hair was fair,
He told me he would always care.
He bought me gifts, gave me flowers,
We would hold hands, and talk for hours.
I thought that he and I would be
Together for eternity.

But then, one rainy day, he left.
I felt heartbroken, and bereft.
I tried to find out where he'd gone,
But he had packed up, and moved on.
I cried for months, I could not see
That our love was not meant to be.
For nights on end, I lay awake,
Thinking there had been some mistake.
A love like ours could not just end,
So surely one day fate would send

My lost love back into my life,
And finally, I'd be his wife.

For many years, I waited for
My love to knock upon my door.
Other men offered me romance,
But I would not give them a chance.
I kept his picture by my bed,
Imagined meeting, in my head.
I bought myself nice clothes to wear,
And dyed the grey out of my hair.
I ate no treats, kept myself slim,
I wanted to look nice for him,
So when we met, he would still see
The young girl from his memory.

And then one day, we chanced to meet!
I saw him walking down the street.
But how he'd changed! I was appalled,
He'd grown quite old, and fat, and bald.
His shoulders stooped, his face was lined,
Nothing about him to remind
Me of the handsome lad I'd known,
For whom I'd spent my life alone.
I watched him pass a homeless man,
He put no money in his can,
Just gave the poor man's dog a kick!
My eyes were opened. I felt sick.

His faded looks I did not mind,
But finding he was so unkind
Had killed the love I'd held so long.
I realised I had been wrong

To wait for him for all those years,
Because he was not worth my tears.
For him, I'd put my life on pause,
I had been blind to all his flaws.

At that moment, he spotted me,
He shouted, "Hi there! Can it be?
It is! It's you! You have not changed,
In all the years we've been estranged.
It's great to see you, and I think,
That we should go out for a drink!"

I stared at him in some surprise,
No recognition in my eyes.
"Oh no," I said, "I'm very sure
That we have never met before."
Then I went to the homeless man,
And put some money in his can.
I stroked the dog, then walked away
From my ex-love, without delay.

I went back home, let myself in,
And threw his picture in the bin.
Then without any time to lose,
I kicked off my smart, high-heeled shoes.
I took off my fine dress of lace,
And wiped the make-up from my face.
I shook the pins out of my hair,
And found something comfy to wear.

Then I rang for a takeaway,
And asked them to come right away

With all the foods I had denied,
Those high in calories, and fried.
I tucked into that lovely food,
And felt a lifting of my mood.
Then after I had eaten that,
Some chocolate cake, high in fat.
I washed it all down with some beers.
I'd not felt so happy in years!

The love I'd craved could never be,
It was all built on fantasy.
And I'd forgotten how to feel
Happiness from things that are real.
The sweetest kiss upon my lips
Can't taste as good as fish and chips!
And now I know, no man can make
Me happy like chocolate cake!

This is a poem about someone who held an opinion that was different to everyone else's...

THE MAN WHO SAID THE WORLD WAS FLAT

The man who said the world was flat,
Was called a nitwit, and a prat.
Anger and insults did abound,
From those who said the world was round.
And so, the man set out to see
If he could prove his theory.

For many weeks, he travelled far,
By bus, and train, and boat, and car.
Until at last he thought he'd found
Proof that the planet is not round.
"Hurrah!" he cried, "I've found the end!
This proves that I'm not round the bend!"
But as he peered over the edge,
Alas, the man fell off the ledge.

It can be hard for a woman to retain her femininity when she has to do DIY...

I USED TO BE A WOMAN

I used to be a woman, but now I'm not so sure.
I'm wearing dirty overalls, sanding down a door.
I used to dress in pretty clothes, feminine, and cute,
But they weren't as practical as this old boiler suit.

I used to be a woman, well made-up, and well dressed,
If you had ever seen me, you would have been impressed.
I used to have such lovely hair, never out of place.
Now I wear a football cap, and paint all down my face.

I used to be a woman, with flowery perfume.
Now it's just the smell of turps that wafts around the room.
One flutter of my eyelashes would drive men insane,
But in these safety goggles, they're fluttering in vain.

I used to be a woman, obvious at first glance.
Young men would rush to date me, if given half a chance.

My dating days are over, I've too much work to do.
The most exciting place I go is to B&Q.

I used to be a woman, but now I'm just a joke.
Most people who see me now mistake me for a bloke.
Other girls have manicures, or sessions at the spa.
I don't seem to have the time - I've got to fix the car.

I used to be a woman. Less useful, I suppose.
Almost good for nothing except powdering my nose.
Now I'm not as feminine as when I first began,
But if something needs fixing, just call me – I'm your man!

This is a tongue-in-cheek poem which I wrote the day after the Brexit result, when many people seemed to be in a state of shock, and there was a lot of confusion and panic about how leaving the EU would affect our daily lives. At the time of writing this, we don't yet know whether Brexit will turn out to be a good thing or a bad thing, but I wanted to end the poem on a positive note...

BREXIT

Britain is leaving the EU!
What happens now? What shall we do?
The pound has dropped right through the floor,
Can't we afford stuff anymore?

Now we've decided that we're out,
Will we still have the Brussels sprout?
Or pizza - that's from Italy?
Or German sausages? Or Brie?

At least we'll still have fish and chips,
And Yorkshire pud, and Walker's crisps,
And that most British food, of course -
Tikka masala curry sauce.

The Scottish people aren't impressed,
They thought that the EU was best.
They may vote to leave the UK,
I hope that they don't go away.

If they leave it will be a shame,
The British flag won't look the same.
I'll miss Scotch eggs, and Scottish ales.
And who gets custody of Wales?

Now, I don't want to seem too mean,
But do we have to keep the Queen?
She is part German, after all,
From Saxe-Coburg, so I recall.

She costs a fortune every year,
Those palaces are far too dear.
Let's give all the Royals the sack,
And let Germany have them back.

From now on, Britain stands alone,
But we are British to the bone.
We'll make the best of what remains,
For Tetley's tea runs through our veins.

There's nothing that we can't create,
Our inventions have made us great -
The World Wide Web, phone, and TV.
I'm sure our best is yet to be!

We'll work hard, go to any length,
We'll eat Hob Nobs to give us strength.

With Sunday roasts, and British beer,
We'll face the future without fear.

Without the EU, we'll survive,
Our Dunkirk spirit will revive.
United we shall stand, and then
We will make Britain Great again.

A long and happy relationship comes to a painful end...

GOODBYE, BED

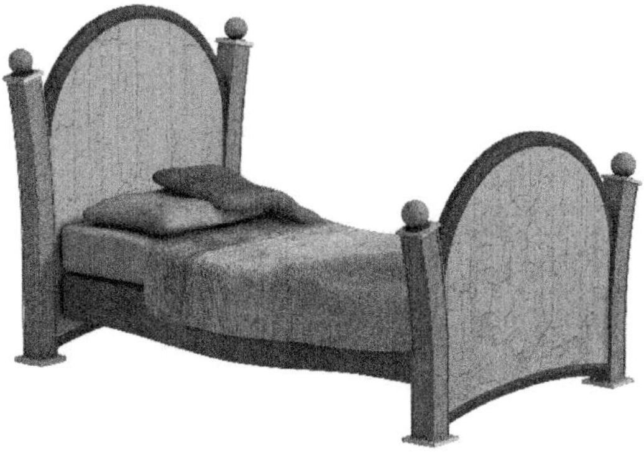

One night, as I got into bed,
And laid to rest my weary head,
I heard a *twang*, and then a *ping*,
And felt my flesh pierced, by a spring.
I fell out of bed with a bump,
For blood was oozing from my rump!

I felt betrayed, and shed a tear
As I stuck plasters on my rear.
I said, "Alas, my deep-sprung friend,
For you and me, this is the end.
We've been pals through bedtime slumber,
Afternoon naps, without number.

We've shared so many pleasant dreams,
You soothed me after nightmare screams.
You held me when I could not sleep,
Secrets, you never failed to keep.

Though lovers came, and lovers went,
You stayed constant, a perfect gent.

There, underneath my eiderdown,
I never thought you'd let me down.
But now it seems you've turned against
Our friendship, and all it once meant.
I did not think the day would come
When you would stab me, in the bum!

Since I can't trust you anymore,
Tonight, I'll sleep upon the floor.
And in the morning, you will see,
I'll pay you back for wounding me.
I'll go down to the nearest store
That's filled with bargain beds, galore.

I'll find a bed that's soft, and kind,
And won't jab me in the behind.
They'll deliver it the same day,
And then they will take you away.
When you have gone, I'll start anew,
With a bed who's *better than you.*"

Next morning, soon as it was light,
I went straight down to Slumber-Rite,
And very soon, just as I'd said,
I had purchased a brand-new bed.
The bed seemed nice, and just the sort
To always give me good support.

They brought the bed round the same day,
And they took the old one away.

I saw them drag it down the stairs,
And said, "Well, good riddance! Who cares!
I'll teach you not to stab my rump,
You're going to the rubbish dump!"

But as they drove away, I fear,
I could not help but shed a tear.
My heart was broken, and I cried,
It felt just like a friend had died,
As with a quiver of my lip,
I watched my bed go to the tip.

I read an article recently which said that many middle-aged people are full of 'anger, disappointment, and dissatisfaction with authority'. It inspired me to write this poem...

I'M A MIDDLE-AGED ANARCHIST

In the depths of suburbia, discontent is brewing.
I thought that I should warn you, so stop what you are doing.
For there is a rising feeling that something's got to give.
It's coming from the middle-aged, no matter where they live.

I'm a middle-aged anarchist! Although it's hard to tell,
I may look ordinary, but inside I'm mad as hell.
You may say it's my hormones, or I'm at a funny age,
But underneath my cardigan, I am burning with rage!

I'm a middle-aged anarchist! A punk, a mutineer,
I'll round up all estate agents, and make them disappear!
I don't want to watch *Bake Off*, or *Strictly*, or *X Factor*.
I don't want to take country drives, stuck behind a tractor.

I'm a middle-aged anarchist! I don't want to drink tea,
I just want to do Jager Bombs all day, till half past three.

I don't want to go food shopping, don't want to stand in queues,
I want to live on takeaways, and chocolate, and booze.

I'm a middle-aged anarchist! A rouser of panic,
I want to eat preservatives, not fresh, or organic.
I want to use a car park, then drive off without paying,
To hell with traffic wardens, and paying and displaying!

I'm a middle-aged anarchist! A rouser of rabble,
I want to drive in bus lanes, I want to cheat at Scrabble.
I want to start a riot, cause political unrest,
I want to march on Westminster, wearing my thermal vest.

I'm a middle-aged anarchist! A rebel with a cause,
I've lived through ten prime ministers, and through the menopause.
I don't want to read newspapers, don't want to watch the news,
I want to streak through Downing Street, in just my comfy shoes!

I'm a middle-aged anarchist! And I'm not giving in,
I don't want to put my recycling in the correct bin.
I want to go to Waitrose, and stand right in the middle,
And shout, "You're being overcharged, it's cheaper at Lidl!"

I'm a middle-aged anarchist! An ignorer of rules,
I'm sick of being sensible, and listening to fools.
I'd lead a revolution, in my Che Guevara cap,
If I just had the energy... I think I need a nap...

Being polite to people can involve having to tell so many lies...

WHITE LIES

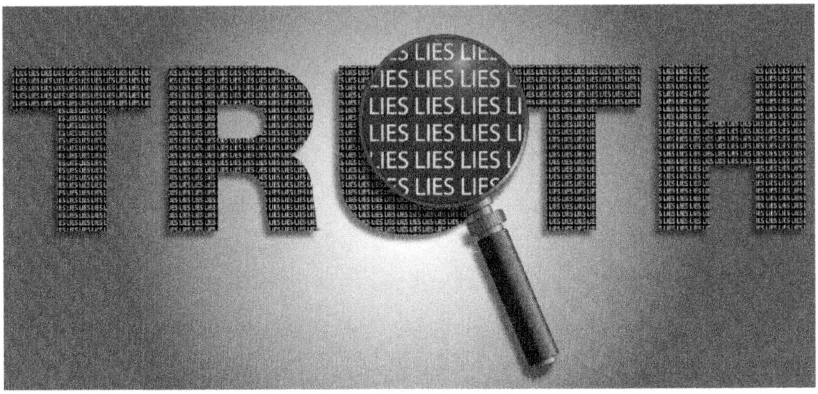

I have something to tell you. I am going to come clean,
I hope that you won't hate me, or think I'm just being mean.
When I saw you this morning, as I took a stroll outside,
I was not quite honest with you. To tell the truth, I lied.

For when you said to me, "Hello! How are you, are you well?"
I answered, "Yes, I'm fine," although I really felt like hell.
But if I'd said, "Well, since you asked, I really feel quite vile."
You would not have wanted to know. You would have run a mile.

When you said, "It's good to see you!" though I said, "Yes, you too!"
I wanted to avoid you, so that was not strictly true.
You see, when I saw you coming, I had an urge to flee,
But you spotted me before I could hide behind a tree.

And when I said to you, "Oh, you look so fab, you look great!"
What I was really thinking is, "You've put on loads of weight."
And when I said, "I truly love what you've done with your hair!"
I really thought, "My god, is that a pigeon's nest up there?"

When you mentioned your husband, I asked, "How is dear old Merv?"
Although, in truth, I can't stand him. I think he is a perv.
At your last Christmas do, he made me wish I had not come,
'Cos when he's had a few, he always tries to pinch my bum.

You bragged about your son, and said he's doing well at school.
But everybody knows that boy's an imbecile, a fool.
I saw the kid last Tuesday, near the corner of our street,
His coat was inside out, and his shoes were on the wrong feet!

You talked about your daughter, and how good she is at art,
But it is common knowledge that girl is a little tart.
The only art she does is spray-painting upon a wall,
"If you're looking for a good time, give my number a call!"

In daily life, we find ourselves telling so many lies,
If folk knew what we really thought, they'd have a big surprise.
We all have our own private views, that we never reveal,
Because we don't want to cause hurt, we care how people feel.

If I told you what I thought of your husband, kids, and hair,
I know you'd be offended, so I won't, because I care.
So I shan't send you this poem, because you are my friend,
And I don't really want to bring our friendship to an end.

Society is built on lies, and it is no one's fault.
If people were all honest, the world would grind to a halt!

Most areas have their own local dishes. This poem is about food that was traditionally eaten in the area I come from. For those who don't know, a faggot is a kind of meatball.

FAGGOTS, BACON AND GREY PEAS

Now, I come from the Black Country, a fact of which I'm proud.
We have the kind of dialect that stands out in a crowd.
But it's not just the way we speak that marks us from the rest.
No, it's also our local food. It's quite hard to digest.

Faggots, bacon and grey peas - tasty and full of fibre.
It's a meal that's sure to please, all for less than a fiver.
You can keep your Yorkshire Puddings, and Devonshire Cream Teas.
Black Country folk like to eat faggots, bacon and grey peas.

Grey peas are good for your heart, they're as healthy as you like.
The trouble is they make you fart, just like a motorbike!
So if you come to try them, I would advise you to bring
A peg for putting on your nose, and a kite on a string!

Faggots, bacon and grey peas, that's the food to set you right.
It's a meal that fills you up, and keeps the bed warm at night.

A dish to keep you regular, and give your bowels ease.
Part your knees - release the breeze! Faggots, bacon and grey peas.

This is a poem about 'empty nest syndrome'...

THE EMPTY NEST

My life was once so full, and blessed,
But now there's just an empty nest.
I was a mum for many years,
I wiped their noses, and their rears.

I coped with chicken pox, and nits,
Toxic nappies, and screaming fits.
The teething, and 'terrible twos',
With stretchmarks, and the 'baby blues'.

I fed them, and taught them to talk,
I watched them learn to crawl, then walk.
I dressed them, and took them to school,
And lessons at the swimming pool.

When they were ill, I was their nurse,
I worried when their coughs got worse.
I got up if they woke to soon,
And dosed them with the Calpol spoon.

I read them stories, played their games,
Remembered all their school friends' names.
I helped them through their teenage years,
The acne, and those 'first crush' tears.

But now my children are all grown,
My chicks have left the nest, and flown.
My husband still has his career,
But I'm redundant now, it's clear.

I've no responsibility,
Just housework, and cooking his tea.
I sweep and mop the spotless floor,
Though footprints aren't there anymore.

The house is too tidy and clean,
It's like an ad for 'Mr Sheen'!
There seems no point in what I do,
I feel so useless, I feel blue.

I wander through each empty room,
The house is silent, like a tomb.
I'm lonely, now I'm not needed.
Thoughts I'd like to share, unheeded.

I resort to conversation
With a talk radio station.
It's not the company I'd pick,
I think the DJ is a dick.

I could look for a new career,
But I am too old now, I fear.

In business, things move on so fast,
My office skills are from the past.

I watch the world go rushing by,
While I stay home alone, and sigh.
Sometimes the highlight of my day
Is when they take the trash away.

One day, I may have grandchildren,
Then I can be useful again!
I'll change nappies, help with weaning,
Once again, life will have meaning.

Till then, I'll sit here, all alone...
But wait, is that the telephone?
My daughter wants to speak to me,
And bring her husband round for tea!

She says they have important news,
Though she won't give me any clues...
It can mean just one thing - hurrah!
A new career - call me 'Grandma'!

In my earlier book, 'Things Can Only Get Verse', I wrote a poem called 'Ted's Love Machine', about a man who bought a fancy car to try to spice up his love life, but unfortunately things didn't go to plan. This is a sequel to that poem...

TED'S BICYCLE

Since Teddy had no luck with cars,
He thought he'd try some handle-bars.
He bought himself a bicycle,
Which he found much more practical.
He rode that bike all round the town,
He rode up hills, then rode back down.
Past stand-still traffic he could race,
And did not need much parking space.

It kept him fit, was cheap to run,
But on his own, was not much fun.
Poor Ted's love life was elusive,
And cycling was not conducive
For giving Teddy half a chance
Of finding meaningful romance.

"Oh dear," said Ted, "What shall I do?
A bicycle's not built for two.
I think my bike would be quite neat,
If it just had another seat...
That idea's not so random,
I just need to build a tandem!
I must try to find out whether
I can weld two bikes together.
That's it!" he cried, "That's what I'll do!
I'll build a love-bike just for two!"

So, Teddy went down to the shed
Belonging to his cousin, Fred.
Fred had an extra bike to spare,
Plus all the tools he needed there.
So Ted worked hard all through the night,
To build a bike that was just right.
And in the morning, he revealed
A love-machine that was two-wheeled.

The bike had got another seat,
And pedals for two extra feet.
A basket full of picnic food,
For dining in romantic mood.
A mini-fridge, to chill champagnes.
A canopy, for when it rains.
A blow-up mattress, and a tent,
(Vital, for a romantic gent!)
Some speakers for his mobile phone,
For music when they're all alone.
And hidden in an inner tube,
A gadget for dispensing lube.

(If you're a rider, you'll know why,
It's no good when your gear's too dry!)

Ted rode his love-bike down the street,
And very soon, he chanced to meet
A pretty girl, called Jenny Hyde,
So he said, "Do you want a ride?"
Jen took one look at Teddy's bike,
And smiling, she said, "If you like."
She climbed aboard, and off they went.
Ted thought this girl was heaven sent.
They rode the bike up Lover's Hill,
Though steep, they pedalled with a will.
They cycled hard with all their might,
It gave them quite an appetite.

At last they reached the highest crown,
And put the picnic blanket down.
They ate the food, and drank champagne,
The day was fine, it did not rain.
Jen's skirt was short, like a pelmet,
She told him she liked his helmet.
When Jen winked, Ted knew what she meant,
It was time to erect... the tent.
Then on the mattress they lay down,
Before they rode back to the town.
They listened to romantic tunes,
Lying together like two spoons.

That night, Ted thanked the skies above,
At last he'd found someone to love!
His love-machine had helped him find
A girl to share his heart and mind.

Ted and Jen are still together,
Riding hard, in any weather.
One day, Jen will become Ted's wife,
Then they'll be in tandem for life.
Each day Ted thanks his lucky stars,
He swapped his car for handle-bars.

I wrote this poem as an entry in a competition, which was to write a crime story in 100 words. I decided to write mine in rhyme...

A BEDTIME STORY

A butcher, married for ten years,
Each night stuffed tissues in his ears,
Because the girl he'd once adored,
All night, just like a piggy, snored.
Well, one night he could take no more,
He went down to his butcher's store,
And fetched his biggest carving knife
To silence his annoying wife.

The knife soon made the snoring cease,
And so at last he had some peace.
His wife was eviscerated,
Snoring noise - obliterated.
He had the best night's sleep in years,
Without her grunting in his ears.
So, the moral of this story -
Don't marry someone who's snore-y.

A poem about domestic unrest...

STRIKE!

After what I found this morning,
I must give you formal warning.
There's no more living as you like,
For I've downed tools - I've gone on strike!

You left the house in such a state,
You'd dirtied every cup and plate,
There's crockery in every room,
Left there to grow a mouldy bloom.

You eat my cooking, and you sup,
But never do the washing up.
If you were asked, I do not think
You could locate the kitchen sink.

Your laundry's all left on the floor,
There's quite a pile behind the door.
Your unwashed socks smell like bad cheese,
They should be sponsored by Febreze!

Now I should not have to ask it -
Put them in the laundry basket!
When I've ironed for half a day,
You could at least put yours away.

A litter bin sits by your chair,
But you don't seem to know it's there.
You drop your rubbish on the floor,
Please be more thoughtful, I implore!

I'm left to do all the cleaning,
How you treat me is demeaning.
You seem to think I am your maid,
But I'm not even getting paid.

If housework really was my job,
I would have quit - you filthy slob!
From now on I would like to see
You give some more respect to me.

Show me some consideration,
Even some appreciation.
Until then, you can take a hike.
Hire a maid - I have gone on strike!

Being a woman of a certain age, I am prone to hot flushes, and all the other symptoms that go with them. So it inspired me to write this poem...

CHANGE OF LIFE

I am a woman at that age
When hormones start to quit the stage.
My oestrogen's gone out the door,
No chance of babies any more.
I'm getting lines around my mouth,
I've put on weight, boobs heading south.
Hair turning grey, and growing thin,
My libido's gone in the bin.

I wake up nightly, drenched in sweat.
My brain feels foggy, I forget.
And through the day, each red-hot flush
Will make me drip with sweat, and blush.
I feel depressed, it's all so weird,
And I've started to grow a beard.
The mirror shows me Santa Claus -
I'm going through the menopause!

It's quite hard not to feel distressed
Knowing that I am past my best.
The menopause is nature's way
Of telling me I've had my day.
Before long, I will reach that age
When I dress head to toe in beige.

No more fun, or youthful ventures,
Just a perm, and plastic dentures.
No more big nights out on the town,
Just bingo, and a nice sit down.
And very soon, I'll have to use
A stair lift, and wide fitting shoes.

Though hot flushes make me feel old,
At least I never feel the cold.
So what I save on heating bills,
I'll spend to ease my other ills,
For women need not age, it seems,
If they buy anti-wrinkle creams.
And hair does not have to be grey,
Hair dye can make that go away.
And I can keep my figure, thanks
To a secret new pair of Spanx!

The menopause is not all bad -
No PMS to drive me mad!
Think positive, things could be worse,
At least there is no monthly curse.
No more cramps, hormonal tension,
Bloating, or water retention.
And I don't need to watch those ads
Where they pour blue liquid on pads,

(You know the ones, where sporty sorts
Play volleyball in tight, white shorts).

So come on ladies, give applause,
Let's celebrate the menopause!

This poem is based on a recent experience I had, when I called a plumber out to fit a new shower. It all took rather longer than I expected...

THE PLUMBER NEVER CAME

Our shower has stopped working! It has given up the ghost.
I shower every morning, just before I have my toast.
But as I washed my hair on Monday, singing, as you do,
It coughed, spluttered, then died, and left me covered in shampoo.

I grabbed a towel, and dripped downstairs, with soap in my eyes,
And searched on my computer for one of those plumber-guys.
I found a few, and called some, asked how much - and then I winced!
They all said they were cheap, although I was not quite convinced.
But then I called a local firm - 'Plumbing for the Thrifty',
The plumber said he'd fit a new shower, for one-fifty.

I asked if he'd come right away, and he said that he would.
He said, "You are in luck today, I'm in your neighbourhood.
Don't you worry, Madam, I will be there in half an hour.
Before you know it, you'll have a brand-new, working shower!"

Well, I waited half an hour. Then I waited four hours more,
But no sign of a plumber's van arriving at my door.
I tried ringing his number, but it just went to voicemail.
I started to suspect that he moved slower than a snail.

I kept trying his number, until at last I got through.
He said he'd been delayed, as he'd had urgent work to do.
He told me that he had to stick just one more bathroom tile,
Then I would be next on his list, he'd see me in a while.

So I waited, and I waited. I waited all that day,
But had no call from the plumber to explain the delay.
When I rang him after six, his voice was filled with sorrow.
He said, "I promise faithfully, I'll do it tomorrow."

So when I rose next morning, to make sure I did not stink,
I had to wash as best I could, while standing at the sink.
Then I stayed home all that day, but the plumber did not come.
I sat there and I waited, till my backside went quite numb!
I called the plumber's number, but did not get an answer.
I started to suspect I was dealing with a chancer!

When finally I spoke to him, as it was getting dark,
He said he'd had an urgent job, near Victoria Park.
He told me not to worry, not think I had been missed,
As early the next morning I'd be first thing on his list.

So I got up the next morning, and washed as best I could,
I used a jug to wash my hair, but it was not much good,
For after I'd finished, I still felt dirty and sweaty.
My hair was limp and greasy - I looked just like a yeti!

I waited in again, but still the plumber never came.
I called to ask him why, and he said he was not to blame.
He had meant to come round, but then his van had broken down.
He'd had to call the AA, from the other side of town.
He said he'd come tomorrow, when his van was on the road.
So I waited in again, but the plumber never showed.

I waited all the next day, then the next day, and the next.
And as you can imagine, I was growing rather vexed!
Well, in the end I gave up. I was weary, I was tired
Of waiting for that plumber - all my good will had expired!

I've called another plumber, though he charges twice the price.
I felt I had no choice, for now I really don't smell nice!
I hope that he is quick. If I don't shower soon, I fear
I'll start to smell so horrible, no plumbers will come near!
I'll turn into a hermit, hide my filthy head in shame,
Embarrassed to go out, because the plumber never came.

Is too much TV bad for relationships...?

VIA SATELLITE

My husband wanted to subscribe to satellite TV.
I said, "Oh, that's a waste of money, you take it from me.
It's just hundreds of channels of stuff you've already seen,
Like *Fools and Horses* on a loop, *Porridge*, and *Mr Bean*."

Well, my husband took no notice - he ignored me, in short.
He went ahead and ordered it, so he could watch the sport.
They came and fixed a metal dish to the front of our house,
To receive enough sports channels to satisfy my spouse.

He sat there and watched football, till his eyeballs went quite square.
You would have thought he had welded his backside to the chair!
He never turned the telly off, all over that weekend.
I soon thought that the satellite would drive me round the bend!

At last, he turned the TV off. He had to go to work.
I thought, "*I'll* never get like that - the silly, square-eyed jerk!"
But then I turned the telly on, to have a little look...
And found a load of channels, just to teach you how to cook!

There's loads of shopping channels, ones for health and fitness too,
Channels just for comedy, and top dramas old and new.
There's loads of documentaries, to really make you think.
I learned how to record things, and to set a series-link.

I found I could pause live TV, or wind forward and back,
And fast-forward through the adverts - it's such a clever hack!
When hubby came back home from work, he had quite a surprise,
I was glued to the telly, and all square around the eyes!

He tried to put the football on, until I shouted, "No!
I am right in the middle of a fascinating show!
I have not cooked your dinner, I've had *such* a busy day,
I spent eleven hours binge-watching *Home and Away!*
You'll have to get a takeaway if you require some grub.
If you want to watch the football - just watch it down the pub!"

That was several months ago, but things are alright now,
We hardly see each other, so we never have a row!
I'm addicted to the telly, I watch all day and night,
I can't seem to turn it off, though I try with all my might.
My husband's always down the pub, though sometimes he must wish
That he had never mentioned getting a satellite dish!

I composed this poem one night, when I couldn't sleep...

WHY CAN'T I SLEEP?

I lie there and watch the bedside clock, for hour after hour.
Although I feel exhausted, sleep is beyond my power.
I've tried counting back from ninety-nine, and reckoning sheep.
Why can't I sleep?

It's not memories of evil deeds keeping me awake.
I *think* I'm a good person, not a villain, or a fake.
Yet I lie sleepless each night, till the dawn begins to creep.
Why can't I sleep?

Is it because I worry about big problems and small,
Like "Did I turn the gas off?" "Is that dry rot in the hall?"
"Should I dispute that garage bill, it did seem rather steep?"
Why can't I sleep?

I'm told hot milk at bedtime is a slumber guarantee,
It does not seem to work on me - it makes me want to wee!
I'm awake *and* my bladder's full, and I just want to weep.
Why can't I sleep?

I purchased a recording that is meant to hypnotise
And render me unconscious, but I hardly close my eyes.
I lie there feeling cheated, till the birds begin to cheep.
Why can't I sleep?

My husband lies beside me, snoring loudly, like a pig.
He does not even notice if I give his ribs a dig.
If I force-fed him this pillow, he would not make a peep...
Why can't I sleep?

Then sometime towards dawn, my tired eyelids begin to close,
My muscles start relaxing, and I fall into a doze.
But just as I start dreaming, the alarm begins to beep!
Why can't I sleep?

I've got to go to work, though I will be too tired to think.
My eyes will look all blood-shot, like I've been out on the drink,
And when the boss is watching, I'll slump forward in a heap,
In a deep sleep.

Not everyone appreciates humorous poetry....

SILLY RHYMES AREN'T A CRIME!

Now, I'm the kind of poetess who tries to make you smile.
I like to write humorous verse, all in a rhyming style.
But some people do not approve of my light-hearted work,
They say I'm not a proper writer - they think I'm a jerk!

They say, "*Your silly verses aren't respectful to the art*
Of writing poetry, 'cos you use words like 'bum' and 'fart'."
They say, "*A proper poem should not make you want to grin,*
And verse that rhymes is childish - it's a faux pas, it's a sin!"

They say, "*You write in language that's too straightforward, and plain,*
Poetry should be confusing, and quite hard to explain.
Real poems sound beautiful, but leave the reader musing,
Open to interpretation, or downright confusing!"

But when folk read my poems, they don't need to summon aid
To decipher the meaning - 'cos I call a spade a spade!
And when a line ends in a rhyme, however it's begun,
I think it sounds much neater, and it makes it much more fun!

So I don't give a toss for those who don't admire my style,
I just can't see what's wrong in trying to make people smile.
Life can be full of problems that will make you frown, and sigh.
You have to see the funny side, or else you'll start to cry.

Serious verse is fine when you want romance and ardour,
In lines that do not rhyme. (Well, writing in rhyme *is* harder!)
But it's well documented that laughter is good for you.
It's just what the doctor ordered, when you are feeling blue.

So when life treats you harshly, and your heart is full of cares,
Try reading some limericks, or some poems by Pam Ayres.
And to all those snobs who think funny rhymes are a disgrace,
I've something serious to say - ***WEE! BUM! FART! SHUT YER FACE!***

Nothing fills me with more fear, than shopping in Ikea...

IKEA

My heart races, I'm filled with fear,
I am trapped inside Ikea!
The store is laid out like a maze,
I wander round for days and days.
The one thing that could set me free
Is an elusive Allen key.
I search under each bed and chair,
But I can't find it anywhere.
And then I wake up with a scream!
And realise it's just a dream...

Not all questions have an answer...

WHY?

There are some things in life that I can never quite explain.
Like, when I peg my washing out, why does it always rain?
When I wait at a bus stop, for what seems like half a day,
Why do I see six buses, all going the other way?
When I'm shopping in a hurry, and join the shortest queue,
Why do people in longer queues get served before I do?

When I wait in for someone, why is there never a doubt,
If I nip to the shop, they'll come and go, while I am out?
Why do all my clothes look so much better on my daughter?
Why does my nose itch when my hands are in soapy water?
Why, when the washing up has all been done, or so I think,
And I empty the bowl - is there a teaspoon in the sink?

Why does the phone always ring when I'm lying in the bath?
Why does other people's litter all end up on my path?
When I shop for clothes and find just what I was looking for,
Why is mine always the one size they don't have in the store?

When I say to a hairdresser, "Please, don't take off too much,"
Why do they never listen, so I end up looking butch?

Why do they call small Mars bars 'fun size'? Small ones are *less* fun!
Why do I go on holiday the one week there's no sun?
Why is there always a 'best man' when a couple get wed?
If he's the best man there, then she should marry him, instead!
When I buy a child a gift, why do they prefer the box?
Why am I always on the toilet when the postman knocks?

I ponder upon all these things, but what makes matters worse,
Is now I'm also wondering - why did I write this verse?

I've worked for some great bosses over the years. And some not so great ones...

OUR BOSS

Who blames others for his mistakes?
And who takes four-hour dinner breaks?
Who won't let us have birthday cakes?
Our boss.

Who has emptied the biscuit tin,
Though he never puts any in?
And whose breath always smells of gin?
Our boss.

Who sits at his desk, fast asleep?
Who is so mean, he makes us weep?
Who is a two-faced, scheming creep?
Our boss.

When we went to the Fox & Hound,
Who was too tight to buy a round,

And said he only had a pound?
Our boss.

Who do we wish would get the sack,
And go away, and not come back?
Who deserves a bloody good smack?
Our boss.

Who thinks he's as smart as can be,
Because he has a PhD
He bought off eBay, for a fee?
Our boss.

Who won't do what he says he will?
Who phones in sick when he's not ill?
Who's taken money from the till?
Our boss.

Who's not as clever as he thought?
Who, to the cops, did we report?
Who will be found 'guilty' in court?
Our ex-boss!

Cooking isn't my strong point. A lot of my food is inedible, though it does have other uses...

CAN'T COOK, WON'T COOK

I'm quite hopeless at cooking, though I try with all my might.
Whatever dish I try to make, it just does not go right.
My rice pudding was horrid, but it did not go to waste,
Although we could not eat it, it made great wallpaper paste!
I tried to bake a baguette, but it came out hard as lead,
Oh well, it came in handy when the leg fell off the bed.
When I made roast potatoes, that did not go well at all.
They turned out like hard bricks, and so I built a garden wall.

No one could eat my rock cakes, they could dislocate a jaw.
So now we use them when we need to prop open a door.
I tried to make some custard, but it ended up like goo,
But still, I found a use. It stuck the heel back on my shoe.
I found a cookie recipe that said 'idiot proof'.
They weren't edible either, but made great tiles for the roof.

So I gave up on cooking, I don't even try these days.
We have all of our meals out, or we ring for takeaways.

Well, now I am too busy to cook dinners, I'm afraid.
I've started my own business - I supply the building trade!

A cut too far...

CURL UP AND DYE

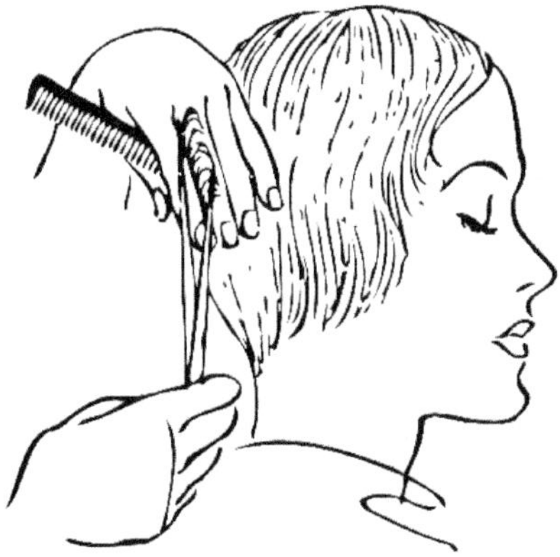

There is a hairdresser's in town,
And they say they won't let you down.
Just pick a style out of their book,
And they'll give you a whole new look.

My neighbour went for a blow-dry,
And asked them for 'The Princess Di'.
She gave the stylist quite a thump,
When it turned out like Donald Trump!

A girl I know went in one day,
And asked them for 'The Beyoncé'.
She left the salon in a rush -
Her hair looked like a toilet brush!

A friend of mine went for a trim,
To make her round face look more slim.
She came out looking like a pig
Wearing a Boris Johnson wig!

My sister said, one of her friends
Asked them to only trim the ends.
When they'd finished, she was appalled,
They'd shaved the lot - she was quite bald!

A girlfriend of my brother, Ted,
Had a big, curly, bushy head.
She hoped they'd make it look littler,
She came out looking like Hitler!

So if you want to change your hair,
I advise you not to go there.
They'll make you look just like a prat.
You'll spend six months wearing a hat!

When being interviewed for a job, it's important to say all the right things...

THE JOB INTERVIEW

Hello, thanks for seeing me. It's a pleasure to meet you!
(To calm my nerves, I'll imagine you sitting on the loo.
Now it's time for the handshake - not too weak, and not too firm,
I wiped it on my skirt first, so my sweat won't make you squirm.)
I've printed out my CV, there's a copy here for you.
(I typed it up last night, and hardly any of it's true.)

You want to know why I'm applying for this vacancy?
Well, I've always admired the work you're doing here, you see!
(Though really, it's because it pays more than my current job,
And I can't stand my boss. I'd like to punch him in the gob.)
You're wondering what skills I have, to fit me for this post?
Well, since you've asked, I'll tell you, though I don't normally boast!

I've had loads of experience doing this sort of work.
I'm punctual and hardworking, I'm never known to shirk.
I'm motivated, and work well alone, or in a team.
(Although, in boring meetings, I am inclined to daydream.)

You want to know where I would like to be in five years' time?
At the top of my profession, as high as I can climb!

My career is important, I'm ambitious, to be sure!
(And when it gets to 5 o'clock, I'm first out of the door.)
I'm not the sort to let an opportunity be missed.
(When it comes to brown-nosing, no bum will be left un-kissed!)
In my spare time, I raise cash for a children's charity,
(Well, I once donated junk to the NSPCC.)

So, thanks for the interview! I'll look forward your call,
When you've seen all of the candidates waiting in the hall.
(When you interview the others, I do hope you won't see
That they're all more experienced, and cleverer than me.)
And if I am successful, just one question - (nervous cough),
I get plastered at weekends, so can I have Mondays off?

Some things in life must be suffered alone...

NO CONVERSATION ABOUT CONSTIPATION

If you suffer constipation,
Your life is filled with frustration.
You spend many hours on your own,
Grunting and straining, on the throne.

Your bum gets welded to the seat,
You lose all feeling in your feet.
It takes you so long to let loose,
You start to feel like a recluse.

It's such a struggle to excrete,
There's teeth marks on the toilet seat.
And it's enough to break your heart,
When all you produce is a fart.

To pass the long hours as you strain,
You use books to distract your brain.
There's time, while waiting for release,
To read the whole of War and Peace.

You will eat old food without fear,
Hoping you'll get diarrhoea.
And if that does not ease your plight,
You're tempted to try dynamite.

It's quite easy to recognize
A sufferer - it's in their eyes.
They look so sad, but then, who smiles
When they're living with chronic piles?

When constipation got him down,
A physician of great renown
Did some research (and I've no doubt,
He used a pen to work it out).

He found that fibre is the cure,
Like wholemeal bread, and fruits galore.
And if that does not ease your bot,
Syrup of figs, and Senokot.

When at last, you're able to do
That long awaited, yearned for poo,
You're filled with such relief and joy,
You feel like shouting, "It's a boy!"

But though you'd like to celebrate
That you've managed to defecate,
You're all alone, there's no one there.
And it's not a thing you can share.

Though pooing's something we all do,
Talking about it is taboo.

It's not acceptable to boast
About it in a Twitter post;

"I've dropped a brown bomb, guys! Woo-hoo!
Happy emoji, hashtag *poo*."
And no one will send you a card,
To say "Sorry your poop was hard."

Toilet talk makes most people blush,
So you just stay silent, and flush.
Your triumph stays for ever more
Hidden behind a toilet door.

This poem is based on an experience I had when I bought a new Christmas tree online. Someone had written a review of the tree, saying "it's so bright, you could see it from space." They weren't joking...

THE NEW CHRISTMAS TREE

Well, Christmas time was almost here, and it occurred to me
That this year I should splash out, and buy a new Christmas tree.
We have an artificial one, lovely when it was new,
But its once silver branches are now tarnished by mildew.
I tried to clean it last year, to remove all trace of mould,
But it would not come off, so now it looks dingy, and old.

So I went on the internet, and found one that looked nice,
A large, green fibre-optic tree, reduced to half the price.
I ordered it, and did not wait long for delivery,
For early the next morning it arrived - my brand-new tree!
I took the tree out of the box to check it was okay,
And had not suffered any sort of damage, on the way.
I removed all the wrapping, stood the tree upon its stand,
And opened all the branches out. I thought it looked quite grand!
I then took the adapter, and I plugged it in the wall,
But when I turned it on - well, I was not prepared at all!

The fibre-optic trees I've seen give a soft, gentle glow.
They shimmer iridescently, like starlight upon snow.
But when my new tree lit up, it was brighter than the sun!
It burned into my eyeballs, like a laser set to stun!
I turned it off, and waited for my vision to return.
It took a while before my retinas had ceased to burn!
I looked at the instructions, and discovered, with a frown,
That there was not a switch so I could turn the brightness down.
There's only two options - turn it off, or let it dazzle,
And wear protection, or you'll burn your eyes to a frazzle!

When Christmas day arrived, eating our lunch was quite a task.
It's hard to eat roast turkey while wearing a welding mask!
When we wanted roast chestnuts, we just hung them on the tree,
And after a few seconds, it had cooked them to a T!
As we gathered round the tree, to do some carol singing,
I think we stood a bit too close - our clothes started singeing!
We all had loads of presents, for when Santa came at night,
He climbed out of our chimney, and was blinded by the light!
He upended his sack, and then he left, quick as he could,
Saying, "Here, just take them all, I don't care if you've been good!"

So if you walk by at Christmas, don't think we are on fire,
Or God has send a bright star, to greet a new Messiah.
It's just our Christmas tree that shines so brightly through the glass,
So if your eyes start burning, please avert them as you pass!
If you would like to buy it, then it's yours for fifteen quid,
But before you plug it in - alert the National Grid!

Every January, we see news stories about how much debt people have got into over Christmas, and about how bad all that Christmas over-eating is for our health. It inspired me to write this poem...

A MERRY CHRISTMAS!
(AND A BANKRUPT NEW YEAR)

Wise men started the Christmas trend
That now drives people round the bend.
They brought myrrh, gold and frankincense,
Which for a baby, makes no sense!
(But in those days, I don't suppose
They had invented babygrows,
And as far as I am aware,
They had not opened Mothercare.)

But since those wise men gave their gifts,
They placed a burden on spendthrifts,
For each year we must do the same.
I really think it is a shame.
We buy friends gifts that they don't need,
And of the cost, we take no heed.

We spend more money than we've got,
And act like we have lost the plot!

The season of gifts and mince pies
Seems to take people by surprise.
It's on the same date every year,
But most don't plan ahead, I fear.
To save for Christmas seems too hard,
It all goes on the credit card.
But then the January bill
Is so big, it makes us feel ill.

We spend a small fortune on food,
To put us in a festive mood.
We eat and drink till we feel sick,
And grow as fat as old Saint Nick.
All that turkey and Christmas pud,
It does not do us any good.
And then we feel compelled to eat
Our own weight in Quality Street.

Why spend more than we can afford,
To show loved ones they are adored?
Why eat till we increase our girth,
To celebrate a baby's birth?
When Christmas is over and done,
We regret all our festive fun.
We're skint, and two stone overweight,
The new year's start does not look great.

This year, give a Christmas greeting,
Without all that over-eating.

And it's time to put an ending,
To our festive over-spending.
For after all, there is no need,
To give in to that yuletide greed.
Be with your loved ones, and give thanks,
Just don't get in debt with the banks!

When you are having one of those days...

TOMORROW IS ANOTHER DAY

When your new phone has stopped working, 'cos you dropped it down the loo,
When you fall into a puddle, 'cos the heel broke off your shoe,
When your parcel did not come, after you waited in all day,
Breathe deeply, and count to ten. Tomorrow is another day.

When you can't pay for your shopping, 'cos you've forgotten your purse,
When you beep at a slow driver, then realise it's a hearse,
When you're bright red with embarrassment, and don't know what to say,
Do not dwell on your mistakes. Tomorrow is another day.

When you've been trying to diet, but find out you've put on weight,
When you missed the bus because you got there a few seconds late,
When you've forgotten the tickets, so you cannot see the play,
Don't give yourself a hard time. Tomorrow is another day.

When your new dress does not fit you, and you can't find the receipt,
When the shoes you thought were comfy gave you blisters on your feet,

When you've got a big zit on your nose that just won't go away,
Try to put on a brave face. Tomorrow is another day.

When someone's ruined your carpet, after walking in dog mess,
When some clumsy fool spills red wine all down your favourite dress,
When your boyfriend has just dumped you, 'cos he's realised he's gay,
Try not to take it to heart. Tomorrow is another day.

When you're locked out of your house because your keys went down the drain,
When you miss an important meeting, 'cos you caught the wrong train,
When you've had the day from hell, and not one thing has gone your way,
It is comforting to know, tomorrow is another day.

Sometimes nothing seems to go right, whatever we try to do,
But after rain, there's always sunshine, to turn those grey skies blue.
When you wake up in the morning, everything will be okay,
For troubles always pass, and tomorrow is another day.

Thank you for reading my book. If you enjoyed it,
I hope you will take a moment to leave a review on the Amazon website.
It would be very much appreciated!

Viv Wade.

About the Author

Viv Wade lives in the Black Country area of the West Midlands, England. She has a husband, a grown-up daughter, and three cats.

Some of her poems are based on personal experiences, some are based on observations, and some are completely made-up. Except the one about the fart-powered hot air balloon - that really happened...

When she is not writing, her hobbies include avoiding people with clipboards, scowling at politicians on TV, and tutting in queues.

She has published another book of humorous poems, *'Things Can Only Get Verse'*, which is available on the Amazon website.